Recess at 20 Below

Cindy Lou Aillaud

To Carmen ~

Always enjoy going outside to Play!

Cindy Lou Aillaud
10-1-05

ALASKA NORTHWEST BOOKS®

Anchorage · Portland

For all the children who opened my eyes
to the possibilities in my own backyard.

A great big hug and thank you to my husband, Whit
and my two sons, Jason and Brian, for always being there with your love,
support, encouragement, and patience. I am also thankful to all
my dear friends that offered assistance when needed. I am forever grateful
to my parents, Ron and Lola May Petett, for sending me outside to play!
A special thanks to all the children who enjoy *Recess at 20 Below*.

Text and photos © 2005 Cindy Lou Aillaud

LIBRARY OF CONGRESS CATALOGING-IN-PUBLICATION DATA
Aillaud, Cindy Lou, 1955-
  Recess at 20 below / Cindy Lou Aillaud.
    p. cm.
  ISBN 0-88240-609-4 (softbound : alk. paper) — ISBN 0-88240-604-3 (hardbound : alk. paper)
  1. Recesses—Alaska—Juvenile literature. 2. Recesses—Alaska—Juvenile literature—Pictorial works. I. Title:
Recess at twenty below. II. Title.

  LB3033.A34 2005
  371.2'424—dc22

                              2005009978

Alaska Northwest Books®
An imprint of Graphic Arts Center Publishing Company
P.O. Box 10306, Portland, Oregon 97296-0306
503-226-2402 / www.gacpc.com

President: Charles M. Hopkins
General Manager: Douglas A. Pfeiffer
Associate Publisher: Sara Juday
Editorial Staff: Timothy W. Frew, Tricia Brown, Jean Andrews, Kathy Howard, Jean Bond-Slaughter
Production Staff: Richard L. Owsiany, Susan Dupere
Editor: Michelle McCann
Design: Andrea Boven Nelson, Boven Design Studio, Inc.

Printed in the United States of America

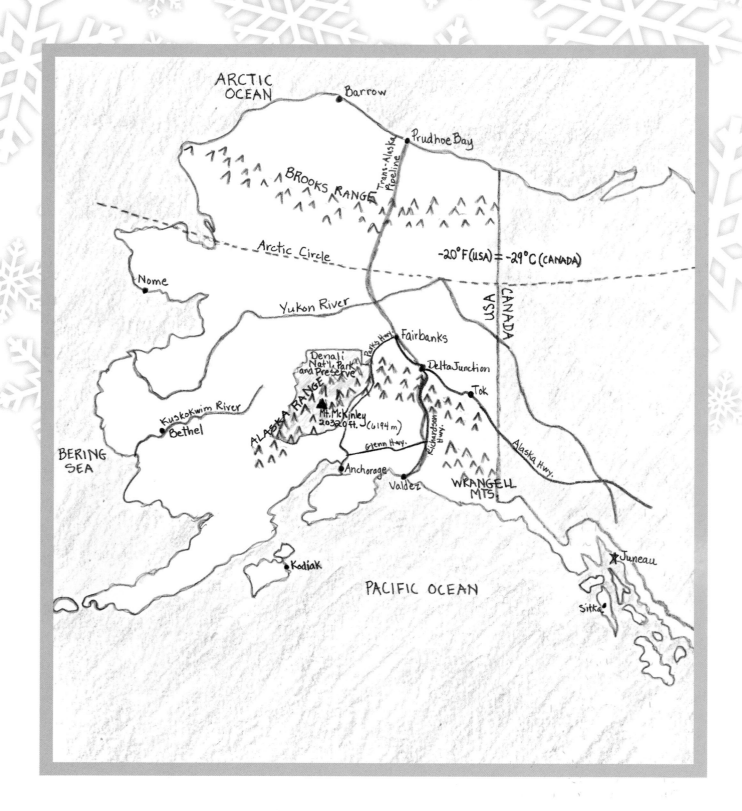

Map by Crystal Finn and Mrs. Aillaud

The cold takes my breath away and makes the inside of my nose stick together, so I tug my scarf up all the way to my eyes. The snow on the ground sparkles like diamonds and the air is filled with tiny ice crystals twinkling out of the sky.

Crunch! Crunch! Crunch! When I walk it sounds like I'm wading through a bag of potato chips. No chance of sneaking up on anyone in this stuff.

I live in Alaska, right along the Alaska Highway. Winter lasts a long, long time here. It seems like forever, but really there's only snow on the ground from September until April. But sometimes we get a snowstorm in May or even in August.

At our school we go out for recess even when it is 20 degrees below zero. We have to wear a LOT of clothes when it gets that freezy.

Getting dressed to go out takes a long time. First, we wiggle and squirm and twist into our thick snow pants. Then we pull on winter boots and zip our parkas as high as the zippers will go—we don't want any cold air getting in.

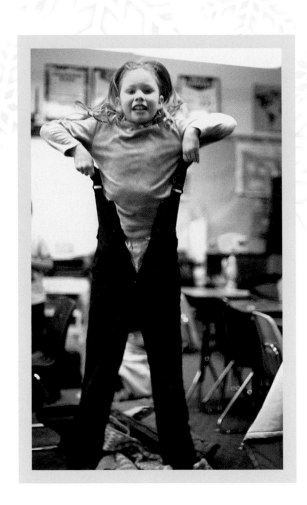

Next come the hats. Some hats cover our whole faces so you can only see our eyes and mouths peeking out. Since we need our fingers to put on all those clothes, our mittens or gloves go on last.

Finally, we're ready to go outside and play. But I can hardly move in all my winter gear—I'm as big as a sumo wrestler! As I waddle down the hall I usually see someone run back to go to the bathroom. Sure hope they make it!

When we get outside I look for my friends. All we can see is each other's eyes, so it helps to remember what colors they are wearing. Samantha reminds me of a giant pickle in her green parka and Megan, who is dressed all in purple, looks like a jar of grape jelly.

It's fun to go sledding during recess. Every time it snows, our maintenance man clears the snow from the school parking lot and dumps it in the middle of the playground. Our sledding hill grows and grows all winter long. After a few months it seems like Mount McKinley (Denali), the highest mountain in Alaska and North America.

We climb to the top and jump on our sleds. *Yippeeeeeeee!*

Sometimes we play on the swings, but by the middle of winter the snow gets so deep there's no room for our legs! We have to throw the swing over the top to make the chains shorter. And the teeter-totters usually freeze to the ground. *Bang! Bang! Bang!* We have to kick them over and over again to break off the ice. Before anyone goes down the slide it is covered with ice crystals that sparkle like glitter. It's like sliding down a glacier.

When it's this cold, we have to be careful never to touch our tongue on something metal. It will stick! Then a teacher will have to use a hair dryer or pour a glass of warm water over it to get your tongue free. How embarrassing!

And snowball fights aren't as easy as you might think where the air is so dry. When it's really, really cold our snow is like powder. We can't even make snowballs, but we like to throw it in the air anyway. We toss up puffy snow clouds and swirling tornadoes.

When the wind blows, the snow gets packed hard and then we can break it into chunks, like giant bricks. We stack the chunks to make forts that go high above our heads. Inside our forts, we keep nice and warm, even when the wind is howling outside.

Sometimes we make tunnels in the snow, too. When we pop our heads out, we look just like bear cubs spying on the action. The only bad part is when the snow goes down our backs while we are tunneling. *Brrrrr*, that's cold!

Some days we play soccer or football during recess. Even at 20 below zero you can get too hot. It's hard work running in big heavy boots and thick snow pants. The more we move the warmer we get.

Playing hard means breathing hard. The moisture from our breath floats up to our faces and makes our eyelashes freeze! They feel so thick and heavy, it's hard to even keep them open. The hair around our faces also gets white with frost, so we look old and gray. Some people say that frozen hair will break if you touch it, but mine never has.

If it's colder than 20 below, we have to stay in for recess. It's too dangerous to be outside then. One day we had to stay inside, but not because it was too cold. We had a visitor on our playground. A moose decided to munch some lunch at our school that day. She came and ate the willow bushes along the fence.

Moose aren't the only wild animals that come to visit. Once I saw a fox sprint through the teeter-totters. Another day ravens attacked our soccer field. Our teacher had drawn some boundary lines with bright red Kool-Aid on the snow. The ravens swooped down out of the sky and gobbled it up!

Our recess is always at noon because it is the sunniest time of the day in my part of Alaska. It isn't very bright though . . . more like early evening. The sun rises and sets in just three hours—it barely peeks above our mountains. We come to school and go home in the pitch-black dark. And if it's cloudy and snowing during recess, the sky gets dark even at noon and it feels like we should get our flashlights out. But it sure makes for good games of hide-and-seek.

By the time the whistle blows to go inside, our cheeks are bright red, our noses are running, and our toes are numb. When we line up we create a cloud of ice fog from everyone breathing in one place. Our breath freezes into tiny specks of ice that hang in the cold air.

*C*lomp! Clomp! Clomp! We sound like a bunch of elephants walking the hallways in our big clumsy boots. When we get to class we peel off our winter gear. Lots of us get wild hair because the air is so dry and our hair is full of static. Sometimes we get big shocks, too, as we pull off our hats. Ouch! It can really zap!